My First Team

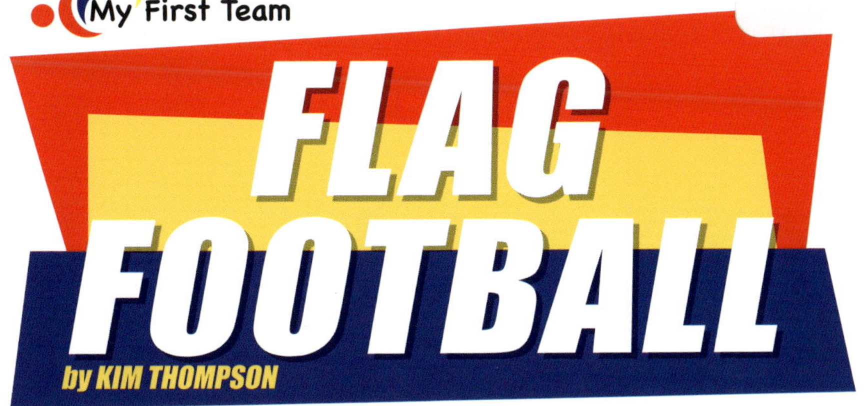

TABLE OF CONTENTS

A Pelican Book

Teaching Tips for Caregivers and Teachers:

Research shows that one of the best ways for students to learn a new topic is to read about it.

Before Reading

- Read the title and predict what the book will be about.
- Read the "Words to Know" and discuss the meaning of each word.
- Read the back cover to see what the book is about.

During Reading

- When a student gets to a word that is unknown, ask them to look at the rest of the sentence to find clues to help with the meaning of the unknown word.
- Motivate students with praise and encouragement.

After Reading

- Discuss the main idea of the book.
- Ask students to give one detail that they learned in the book.

SIGHT WORDS

a	not	up
are	over	want
do	play	we
get	the	
give	to	

WORDS TO KNOW

catch

flag football

line

team

throw

We play **flag football**.

flag football

We **throw** the football.

throw

catch

We **catch** the football.

We do not want to give up a flag.

We want to get the football over the **line**.

line

We are a flag football **team**!

team

Index

Written by: Kim Thompson
Design by: Jen Bowers
Series Development: James Earley

Photos: cover and p.11 ©2020 Stuart Monk/Shutterstock; p.4-5 ©2020 Stuart Monk/Shutterstock; p.6 ©2019 Torychemistry/Shutterstock, ©2021 JoeSAPhotos/Shutterstock; p.7 ©2020 JoeSAPhotos/Shutterstock; p.8 ©2020 JoeSAPhotos/Shutterstock; p.9 ©2008 Amy Myers/Shutterstock; p.10 ©2018 JoeSAPhotos/Shutterstock; p.13 ©2018 JoeSAPhotos/Shutterstock; p.15 ©2006 Gary Paul Lewis/Shutterstock

Library of Congress PCN Data
Flag Football / Kim Thompson
My First Team
ISBN 978-1-63897-417-8 (hard cover)
ISBN 978-1-63897-532-8 (paperback)
ISBN 978-1-63897-647-9 (EPUB)
ISBN 978-1-63897-762-9 (eBook)
Library of Congress Control Number: 2021953266

Printed in the United States of America.

Seahorse Publishing Company
www.seahorsepub.com

Published in the United States
Seahorse Publishing
PO Box 771325
Coral Springs, FL 33077